IMAGES OF ENGLAND

RIPPONDEN
AND THE RYBURN VALLEY

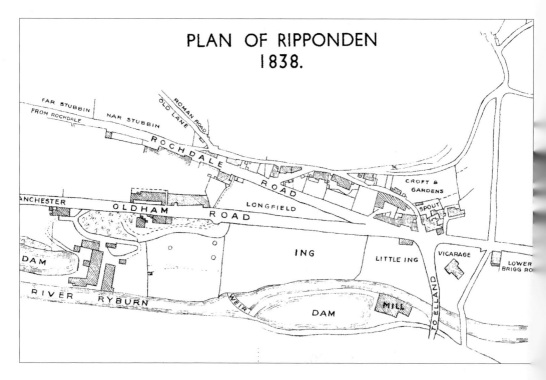

PLAN OF RIPPONDEN
1838.

IMAGES OF ENGLAND

RIPPONDEN
AND THE RYBURN VALLEY

DAVID CLIFF

TEMPUS

Frontispiece: This is the logo of the former Ripponden Urban District Council, which was formed in 1937 on the amalgamation of the former Soyland, Rishworth and Barkisland councils. Ripponden UDC was itself swallowed up by the formation of Calderdale Metropolitan Borough Council in 1973. Ripponden Parish Council was formed at the same time and continues to use the same logo with the necessary changes to the wording and date. The logo depicts the old packhorse bridge over the river Ryburn.

Map from 'Ripponden and the Spout', by J.H. Priestley, Halifax Antiquarian Society Transactions, 6 June 1942. John Priestley, who lived at Carver Clough, Rishworth, has written many papers on the local area for the above Transactions.

First published 2007

Tempus Publishing
Cirencester Road, Chalford,
Stroud, Gloucestershire, GL6 8PE
www.tempus-publishing.com

Tempus Publishing is an imprint of NPI Media Group

© David Cliff, 2007

British Library Cataloguing in Publication Data.
A catalogue record for this book is available from the British Library.

ISBN 978 0 7524 4412 3

Typesetting and origination by NPI Media Group
Printed in Great Britain

Contents

Acknowledgements

First and foremost I have to thank Tracy for being so patient during my long vigils at the keyboard during the last few months and for keeping me well supplied with coffee and biscuits. Secondly I have to thank all those photographers, both amateur and professional, who went out with their cameras to record the local scene for us; without them this book would not have been possible.

I have to thank Donald Taylor for giving me free access to his wonderful collection of local postcards and for his personal anecdotes. Hazel Whiteley also let me borrow from her extensive collection of photographs and local history notes. Her interest in local history is well known (see the bibliography at the end of the introduction) and hopefully her planned history of Ripponden will come to fruition. Others who have assisted are: Sheila Shepherd (Rishworth School), Gary Walton, Michael and Margaret Crawshaw, Graham Crawshaw, Liz Moss, Dorothy Mellors, Sue Neave and Ripponden Parish Council.

I also have to thank Heather Karpicki and the ladies at Sowerby Bridge Library for their help in accessing the wonderful local history collection held there. The photographs used from the library collection are reproduced with the permission of Calderdale MBC Libraries, Museums and Arts. Every effort has been made to contact copyright owners; however it has not been possible to determine the copyright status of all the photographs used; should copyright holders come forward after the publication of this book then a full acknowledgement will be given in future editions.

I thank everyone who has assisted me in the preparation of this work: without your help this book would not have been possible.

Introduction

My 2006 book on Sowerby Bridge also covered the lower end of the Ryburn Valley as far as Triangle. The story now continues along the rest of the valley to the county boundary at Windy Hill (M62) and Blackstone Edge.

The title of this series is 'Images of England' and this focuses our attention on the period after 1860, when photographers, happily for us, were going about recording local scenes with the rudimentary cameras of the day. It may, however, be of interest to readers for me to add a few notes on the history of Ripponden and the Ryburn Valley.

We know that ancient man lived in the area: the stone circle at Ringstone, Meg Dyke earthwork at Scammonden, and other finds, such as worked flints, on the hill tops around the valley are proof of this. The Brigantes tribe occupied this part of Britain at the time of the Roman invasions and the latter have also left their mark on the area – for example, a hoard of Roman coins has been found in Mytholmroyd and a Roman altar bearing the date AD 208 has been discovered at Greetland. A Roman road crossed the Pennines at Blackstone Edge and continued down past Baitings, along Blue Ball Road, descended to the valley floor via Ripponden Old Road, crossed the river near the present packhorse bridge and continued up Old Bank to Greetland. Historians are generally in agreement with this but the jury is still out on whether the paved causeway section at Blackstone Edge is Roman or whether the road surface was improved in the later medieval or Tudor periods.

Local place names date largely to what might be termed the early medieval period. 'Ripponden' has been spelt in a variety of ways over the centuries but one old version, 'Ryburnedene', is translated as, 'the crossing (or ford) of a river in a wooded valley'. 'Rishworth' is where the 'rushes were kept or stored'; 'Barkisland' is 'the land of the birch trees'; and 'Soyland' means 'south land' signifying its location in relation to Sowerby of which it was originally part. In the medieval period the area was owned from 1116 by the Warrens (Earls of Surrey) and later by the Savile family.

The river Ryburn was the boundary between Barkisland and Soyland and the old village of 'Ripponden' was located on the Barkisland side of the river around the church, which was first built by a Royal Grant of 1464. The first mention of a bridge is from 1313, and at that time a water-wheel-driven fulling mill, (pounding wet cloth to 'full' or felt it), was operating nearby, probably on the site of the later Ripponden Mill. A tax assessment of 1284 charged Sowerby and Soyland sixteen shillings, Barkisland ten shillings and Rishworth eleven shillings.

During the sixteenth, seventeenth and eighteenth centuries, what is termed the 'domestic system' of making cloth developed: the land was too poor to make a living from farming alone, so when it was fine the farmer would work on the land and when it rained he wove woollen cloth on his hand loom. As the trade developed merchant clothiers such as Samuel Hill at Making Place,

Soyland, made their fortunes by supplying the raw wool and buying up the pieces of cloth to sell on in bulk. By the eighteenth century the clothiers were building water-driven mills along the rivers and streams where they employed a workforce to produce the cloth; the home weavers couldn't compete and were forced to migrate to the valley bottoms to find work in the mills.

The greatest boost to the local economy came in the eighteenth century with the building of the two turnpike roads through the district; the 1770s Rochdale to Halifax and Elland road (A58); and the 1803 road from Oldham to Ripponden (A672). This resulted in the development of the main part of the modern village on the Soyland side of the river, especially during the later Victorian period.

Cotton was introduced to the area at the end of the eighteenth century, no doubt as a result of the new road links with Lancashire, and cotton spinning would soon almost replace the wool trade in the Ryburn Valley; not entirely, as there were still a few mills processing wool and silk and making paper. Water wheels were gradually replaced by steam engines using coal easily shipped in after the opening of the Rishworth Branch railway line. In his 1933 paper, J.H. Priestley lists thirty-seven known mills in the valley and its side valleys, although these were not all operating at the same time.

Ripponden Co-operative Society was founded in 1832 and is claimed to be the oldest in the country; members of the society were also instrumental in establishing the Commercial Mill Company in the 1850s.

Each of the three townships – Soyland, Barkisland and Rishworth – conducted their own affairs and elected their own parish officials. In 1863 Barkisland and Rishworth became Local Boards of Health, followed by Soyland a year later. Soyland became an Urban District Council in 1895, meeting at Stones School. It will be noted that Soyland UDC covered the main part of Ripponden while Barkisland covered the old part of the village on that side of the river. This anomaly was rectified in 1937 when all three were combined to form Ripponden UDC.

The trams from Halifax only ever reached as far as Triangle, resulting in the train service to the higher reaches of the valley being well patronised for many years. The railway began to suffer however from the introduction of road transport in the early twentieth century and eventually had to close when it became uneconomical to continue. One such local road transport firm was Ripponden & District Motors, who started out as bus operators and later moved on to parcel delivery, becoming one of the biggest employers in the valley.

In 1973, Ripponden UDC was swallowed up with the formation of the larger Calderdale Metropolitan District Council. Ripponden was given Parish Council status and that body continues to look after the interests of the people of the valley. The Parish Council still use the same logo of the packhorse bridge as the former Ripponden UDC.

Today there are no textile mills still operating in the valley, the railway has gone and so has Ripponden & District Motors. The valley has recovered from the pollution of the industrial age, the tree cover has increased, the river is clean and the vegetation now thrives, no doubt partly due to global warming. It remains a walker's paradise of moorland, woodland and riverside paths with history around every corner. No wonder the Calderdale Way passes through the village and the Pennine Way skirts the old Rishworth Township boundary.

For further reading I would recommend *The History of Ripponden* by John H. Priestley, 1903; *Ryburn Tapestry* by Hazel Whiteley, 1975, and Hazel's *Ripponden History Trail*, 1986, which is still available from the Parish Council Office. Two other books which give a fascinating insight into life in the valley are edited by Jean Mallinson Akroyd – *Ryburn Valley Reflections* (1991) and *Further Reflections from the Ryburn Valley* (2001).

David Cliff
Ripponden 2007

one

The Village Centre

This fascinating old view is probably the oldest photograph of Ripponden, dating from around 1865. It's hard to imagine today how polluted the atmosphere was in those days with the mill and house chimneys pouring out smoke. On the left is Chapel Field Mill and Ripponden Mill (which burnt down in 1876) is in the centre. The Junction Inn stands alone to the right of Ripponden Mill. The old church was taken down in 1868 and replaced by the present one.

Compare this scene of 1900 with the one above – what a difference thirty-five years make! The new Ripponden Mill has replaced the one burnt down in 1876 (the new mill burnt down in 1980) and Chapel Field Mill appears to have installed a lift shaft. The centre of the village is filling up with shops and housing and the Junction Inn no longer stands alone.

View from Maude Lane looking up Elland Road, *c.* 1909. Chapel Field Mill burnt down in 1929 when the children from the school across the road were evacuated and allowed to watch the blaze from the hillside. Above the school can be seen Ripponden railway station with the railway bridge over Elland Road.

The centre of Ripponden from Height Walk, with Ripponden Mill and its dam. The dam was later drained and is now the recreation ground. The abattoir is at extreme left and Central Garage occupied the sloping field site until recently.

Old Ripponden Bank, *c.* 1900. The cottages on the left were built by Richard Jackson in the late 1700s and were bequeathed to the church in 1914, to become the Community Centre. The white building next door is the Black Lion Inn and beyond that further up on the same side of the street is the old white building of the Canterbury Inn (the Old Cant). When the Ripponden railway station was opened the landlord of the Canterbury changed its name to The Railway Hotel (closed 1906). Silver Street leads off uphill to the left. The large central building is The Chartists Hall (or Foresters Hall) where the local Chartists held their meetings; dances were also held here for the cotton workers from Ripponden Mill.

A closer view of the buildings on the right of the previous photograph. The building on the left has a tobacconist's sign above the door. The small room over the archway was once the home of Tommy Stott, the churchwarden. Beneath the archway steps led down to Cob Clough, the village's main water supply, known as the 'parish pump'. Cob Clough is then channelled under the road and graveyard to empty into the river near the packhorse bridge. The building on the right later became the Ryburn Farm Museum.

Above: The Ryburn Farm Museum, which was opened in 1975 by the Ryburn Civic Trust, recreated the living and working quarters of a farming family in the mid-nineteenth century. The museum closed in 1990. Photograph by Roy Dyson, 1975.

Below: Lilywhite postcard of the old packhorse bridge with the Bridge Inn and the vicarage beyond. First mention of a bridge here was in 1313 and the first stone bridge was built in 1533. The bridge was scheduled as an ancient monument in 1934 and as a listed building in 1966. The vicarage was built by the Revd John Watson, vicar of Ripponden from 1754 to 1769.

Left: Old Bank, *c.* 1940. This community constable is from the West Riding Constabulary and probably worked from the police station that occupied the right-hand side of the White Swan pub (now the Pekin restaurant). He is standing with Albert Taylor who lived at Fielding Farm behind them. Mr Taylor was a pig farmer and also worked at William Bottomley's cotton mill in Ripponden.

Below: No, not a scene from a well-known brown bread commercial, but another view of Old Bank below and round the corner from the previous view. All these buildings have now gone.

Elland Road, looking up towards the Golden Lion, *c.* 1905. The road does lead up to the former railway station and may have been known locally as 'Station Road'. The nearest shop is that of Joseph Mellor – 'Practical Printer, Stationer, Newsagent and Bookbinder'. The girl is standing outside John Holden's grocery shop. The buildings behind the Golden Lion have now gone.

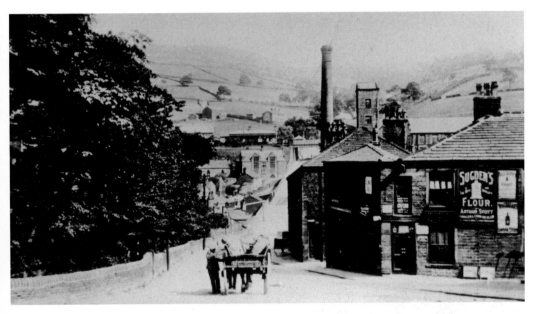

View looking up Elland Road towards the national school and railway station *c.* 1917. The chimney and lift-tower belong to Chapel Field Mill. The shop of Arthur Stott, grocer and corn dealer is on the right with the advert for Sugden's Flour.

Above: Ripponden centre, *c.* 1910. Note the horse omnibus outside the Golden Lion. At this time the extension to the front of the pub housed a reading room over stables. Ripponden centre was lit by gas lamps from 1882. On the right is the 'Crystal Palace' on the site of the old toll house. The large building behind the trees is the Conservative Club, built in 1899.

Above: Looking towards Triangle from the top of Elland Road, *c.* 1948. The Golden Lion is now selling Whitaker's 'Cock o' the North' Ales. Note the row of wooden huts beyond, the middle one appears to be tobacconists; a block of flats now stands on this site, but the tree survives. Note also the guidepost (1768), bottom right – the names were chiselled off at the beginning of the Second World War so that the Germans would get lost when they arrived!

Right: One of the huts in the view above was Nathan Whiteley's 'Tripe Restaurant' where fresh supplies of pie and peas and tripe were delivered daily. It was at one time 'Bentley's Tripe Restaurant'. In around 1900 another of the huts was a doctor's surgery!

Opposite below: Arnold Butterworth's greengrocery shop can also be seen on the left of the previous photograph in the sloping-roof extension of the Queen Hotel. He was also a fish dealer and according to the sign, orders were 'promptly executed'.

Postcard view of the centre of the village looking towards Rishworth. The 'Crystal Palace' is on the left. The village stocks once stood near to where the boy is sitting on the wall.

Ripponden cattle market was held on the first Tuesday in April on the space created by the demolition of the protruding wing of the Golden Lion. The awning on the shop behind advertises Southwell's drapery and millinery business; the shop is now a chemist's.

Looking up Rochdale Road from the centre of the village, *c.* 1906. On the left is the 'Crystal Palace'
which stands on the site of the old toll-bar house. When the height of the building was increased the
top storey was designed to look like the original toll building; it was occupied after the Second World
War as the headquarters of the local Labour Party. At the time of the photograph the premises were
being used by Mitchell & Son Auctioneers who bought it in 1873 when the tolls were abolished.
Later on, when the glass windows had been walled in, it became a branch of the Bank of Liverpool.

Top hats are amongst the headgear being worn by this group outside the Queen Hotel. The sign over
the doorway to the right of the hotel reads 'Good Stabling'. The figure fourth from the right appears
to be a police officer wearing the kepi headgear. The little girl is standing outside the small shop of the
local clock maker, Thomas Whiteley, known as 'Tom Clock'. The business was still going in the 1930s
and was owned by Roland Howarth. Note the horse omnibus standing outside the Golden Lion.

Above: This is a similar view to the last photograph but worthy of being reproduced to show the mode of transport of the period. The sign over the door of the shop to the left of the Queen Hotel shows it to be the post office, probably at that time being run by Miss Bradley, daughter of the landlord of the Queen Hotel. In the 1860s meetings both for and against the railway were held at the Queen Hotel and it was the stopping place for the Liverpool to Halifax stagecoach.

Left: A rather faded old photograph but full of period charm. 'Fred Berry – Baker and Confectioner' occupied the shop to the left of the current newsagents and post office. As well as providing teas and refreshments, the shop also sold bride and funeral cakes, and was noted for its veal pies.

Opposite above: Village centre, some time in the 1920s. The Queen Hotel has now been clad in its mock-Tudor timbering. The motor age has arrived. The wagon on the left is parked outside the branch of the Sowerby Bridge Industrial Society.

Below: Sowerby Bridge Industrial Society had their No. 1 branch in what is now the newsagents. The building was erected in 1863 on the site of the old smithy. The shop to the right is now incorporated into the newsagents as the post office section but at the time of the photo (around 1907) it was the shop of W.H. Broadbent, newsagent.

Postcard view of the village centre. The street scene was to change dramatically in 1971 when traffic lights were installed at the junction of the A58 Rochdale and the A672 Oldham Roads.

Opposite above: Village centre in the 1920s. Businesses along the right-hand side of the street are (from left to right): the Liverpool Bank; clock repair shop; Garsides ironmongers; Beaumonts service depot; clothing shop; Hollas, fruiterers, fishmongers and poultry dealers; Lumbs, pharmacist; post office. The Garsides building later became a branch of Lloyds Bank, which closed in 2006, Ripponden's last bank.

Opposite below: View, *c.* 1900. The pram is outside C. Garside & Sons, plumbers and ironmongers. At this time, F.W. Sutcliffe & Co. Ltd were running the pharmacist's shop. Besides surgical goods and medicines, they also specialised in cameras and films, and perhaps someone from the shop took this photograph.

Closer view of the row of shops at the junction of Rochdale and Oldham Roads with Sutcliffe's on the left, the post office in the centre and Whiteley's tobacconists on the right.

Above: Postcard sent from Halifax to Miss Annie Stott at Clay Pitts Farm, Soyland, possibly 1911.

Below: Lilywhite postcard addressed to a patient in bed No. 12, Rawson Ward, Royal Halifax Infirmary but never completed or posted.

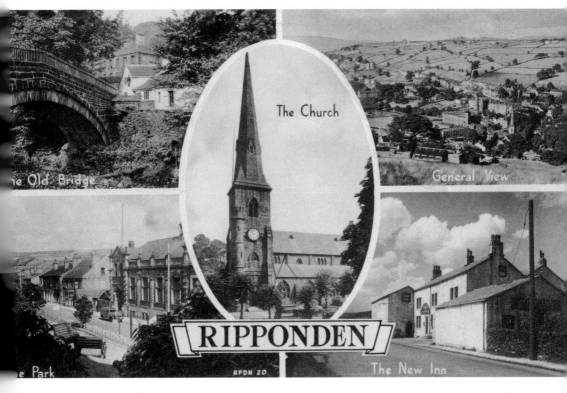

The Old Bridge

The Church

General View

RIPPONDEN

RPDN 20

The Park

The New Inn

Spring Street, Ripponden, clearing up after the flooding caused by a torrential downpour in 1947. Water rushed down Ripponden Old Lane carrying mud and rocks. The buildings on the right have now gone, as has the communal water pump which once stood in the street. The Working Men's Club was once located at Stoops Farm at the bottom of the street, but in 1887 it moved to new premises in Rochdale Road (now the chapel of rest).

A winter scene in Ripponden. Possibly the 1940s.

Pleasant Row in Oldham Road, also known as Co-op Row as it was here that Ripponden Co-operative Society started up in business in 1832. The society eventually purchased the whole row. No doubt Mr Stringer was kept busy in those days when footwear was meant to last and was repaired when required.

Brig Royd House, Ripponden, was built between 1806 and 1840 by Richard Howarth, a local lawyer. The site had previously been a farm. The last occupant was Mrs Robina Ayres and after her death the estate came into the ownership of Ripponden Urban District Council who built housing, a doctor's surgery and a library. The old house was demolished and the site is now occupied by Brig Royd Old People's Community Centre. ⎯ Where Emma Had 100th Birthday Party

Ripponden war memorial shortly after being erected. The memorial bears the names of sixty-two local men who died in the First World War, and a further eighteen who died in the Second, 'For Peace and Freedom'. War memorials at Rishworth and Barkisland remember the men from those districts who also gave their lives.

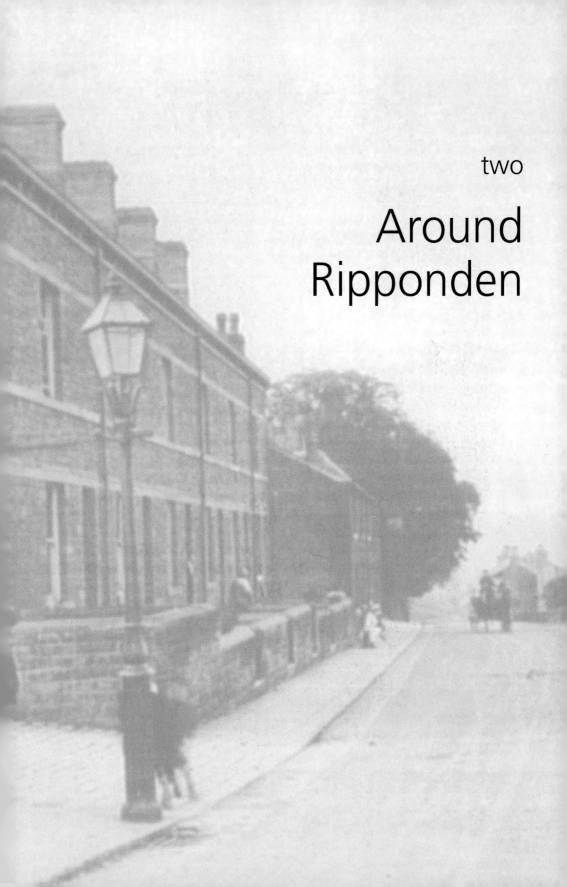

two

Around
Ripponden

Wood Terrace, Halifax Road, Ripponden, *c.* 1910. Typical of the small shops that were such a feature of the area is this baker and confectioner's advertising malt bread. It is now a private house.

Cliffe Cottage, Halifax Road, Ripponden. Now called Ryecliffe House.

This part of Kebroyd Hall was built in around 1840 by the Hadwen family, silk spinners of Kebroyd Mills. In the mid-eighteenth century the site was owned by Samuel Hill of Making Place and he built a house here for his son Richard, part of which still stands to the right of this photograph. Richard was later disinherited by his father.

This is Whiteley Gee's grocery and confectioner's shop in Halifax Road, Kebroyd. He formally worked for the Ripponden Co-operative Society at their Rishworth store, but left in 1928 to open his own business here. The shop closed in the 1970s and is now a private house.

Postcard of Halifax Road, Kebroyd looking towards Denton Bridge. The cottages on the left of the road have now been demolished. The postcard was written from 'Vera' to 'Bessie Earnshaw' in Blackpool – 'Many thanks for the post-card which I have just received, I like it very much. I am enjoying myself very much, glad to hear that you are doing the same'.

Alexandra footbridge replaced the stepping stones over the river Ryburn at Kebroyd prior to 1913. The bridge would have been used by walkers to reach Little Haven and Norland.

LITTLEHAVEN Tea Gardens, Kebroyd nr. Triangle.

RIPPONDEN.   KEBROYD.   TRIANGLE.   SOWERBY BRIDGE.   HALIFAX.

Leafy Walks

Littlehaven Tea Gardens

Riverside Beauty

TOBACCO, CIGARETTES,
REFRESHMENTS,
NEW LAID EGGS. POULTRY.

CAMPING GROUNDS.
WEEK-ENDS AND HOLIDAYS.
PARTIES CATERED FOR.

Tea Gardens

Flowery Ways

ENJOY A PLEASANT AFTERNOON
OR EVENING IN THE PRETTIEST PART
OF YORKSHIRE'S PRETTIEST VALLEY.

Magnificent Scenery

Little Haven is situated in the woods above Denton Bridge on the Norland side of the valley at Kebroyd. It was once a very popular visitor spot where you could 'enjoy a pleasant afternoon or evening in the prettiest part of Yorkshire's prettiest valley'. Besides the tea gardens, camping was allowed and tobacco, cigarettes, refreshments, eggs and poultry could be purchased. Today it is a private house.

Farmer Kershaw at Flat Head Farm, Soyland. The date is unknown but the calendar shows it is January and no doubt Mr Kershaw is enjoying the warmth from his Yorkshire range.

The Royd, Royd Lane, Soyland. Royd is an Anglo-Saxon word meaning a man-made clearing in a wood. In the early 1700s, The Royd became the property of John Hoyle and later, by marriage, to Robert Allenson, who with his nephew, James Hoyle, manufactured woollen cloth at Ripponden Mill. Robert Allenson built the mansion at Royd, in a style foreign in character to other local houses.

Thrum Hall (also known as Beeston Hall or Beestonhurst), near Gig Mill, Rochdale Road, Ripponden, c. 1900. John Royds born here in the 1700s founded one of the first banks in Halifax. He built and lived in Somerset House in George Square, Halifax, which is still there but has now been converted into several shops, a café, a pub and a bank.

Rochdale Road at its junction with Castle Lane on the left and Dyson Lane on the right, although this whole area was once referred to as Dyson Lane. The photograph can be dated to 1906-9, as Dyson Lane Mill on the right is in the process of being demolished. A row of terraced houses was later built on the site, the end house of which, nearest the camera, became a branch of the Ripponden Co-op.

This block of four cottages stands in Rochdale Road just above Stones church. The shop closed a long time ago and is now a private residence. It is probably the shop referred to in the history of Stones church and school – 'Many a scholar has peered into the sweet shop of Mrs John Parker, Stones, and longed to spend their school pence'. The photograph was taken c. 1910.

Row of houses above Gig Mill, Rochdale Road, *c.* 1910. The barn at the right-hand end has now been converted into a house.

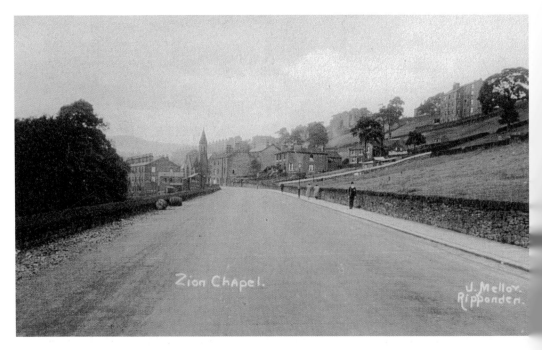

View along Oldham Road with Zion Chapel in the distance. Houses now cover the fields on the right.

Holroyde's Furnishing Warehouse in Oldham Road, apparently also an ironmongers, judging by the shovels, spades etc. in the window.

Taken just to the left of the above photograph, this one shows the workshop of the business – 'J. Holroyde & Sons, Cabinet Makers and Upholsterers'. The firm was started by Joseph Holroyde, whose family once lived at Chapel House Farm. The Holroydes were also butchers (see the adverts on p. 24). The premises are now used by a local potter.

The three-storey cottages, bottom left, in Oldham Road were once a small textile mill known locally as 'T Shoddy'. In the early 1800s it was used as a weaving shop by John Edwards, producing cheap woollen cloth woven from recycled yarn. To the right can be seen the Zion Chapel. The area in the bottom left-hand corner later became part of Ripponden & District Motors' garage site.

View looking down the valley from above Stones House. In the centre is Commercial Mills with Rishworth railway station on the right. The spire of St Bartholomew's church can be seen in the distance.

three

Barkisland

This block of houses is called Fairview and still stands in Ripponden Bank opposite the Fleece Inn. At the time the photograph was taken in around 1900, the middle house was a shop run by Richard Gee. Note the variety of windows. When the shop finally closed it reverted to being a house once again.

Barkisland Hall is a grade I listed building, the highest ranking that any building can have. Thomas Gledhill was one of the largest taxpayers in the township and had been granted a coat of arms in 1612. Barkisland Hall was built in 1638 by his son John, who married Sarah Horton, daughter of William Horton of the Howroyde. Above the door is a carved head, heraldic crest and coat of arms as well as the initials of John and Sarah Gledhill. The hall was once owned by Lord Kagan, who made his fortune from his Gannex raincoat, produced at his factory in Elland. The Prime Minister, Harold Wilson, was a visitor to the hall during that period.

The Howroyde was the seat of the Horton family and the manor house was rebuilt by William Horton in 1642. A grade I listed building, it stands in a wooded estate where once deer roamed free. Over the fireplace in the hall is the royal coat of arms of Charles I, placed there at the time of building and for which privilege the king extracted a fee of ten shillings. Until recently it was the home of Richard Thorpe, who plays Alan Turner in the TV soap *Emmerdale*. One distinguished visitor in the 1940s was Ivor Novello, who, while staying there, wrote his best-known song, 'We'll Gather Lilacs in the Spring Again'.

Barkisland stocks still stand in the main village street outside the north wall of the old Barkisland lock-up (prison). The latter is now a private house with a rare witches post. This photograph is from a postcard dated 1906. Stocks were used to punish drunks and vagrants and another set survives in nearby Norland.

Members of Barkisland Urban District Council and their wives on an excursion, *c.* 1900. The tree in the background is believed to be the Major Oak in Sherwood Forest, Nottinghamshire. In the back row (from left to right): Mr Horsfield (solicitor), William Darby (keeper at Ringstone Edge Reservoir), Elijah Lee, Frank Bottomley, Zachariah Taylor, William Clark (schoolmaster at Barkisland), Richard Clements (surveyor), Dr Hoyle. At the extreme left of the middle row is Mr George Hewitt (Ripponden schoolmaster) and at the other end is Mrs Z. Taylor. On the extreme left of the front row is Mrs Hewitt and next but one to her is Mrs Darby. The Urban District Council was formed in 1895, replacing the old Local Board which had been set up in 1863.

The Krumlin Pop Festival, August 1970. Groups who appeared included Pink Floyd, The Who, The Kinks and Manfred Mann, with a surprise appearance from Jimi Hendrix. After this photograph was taken, torrential rain and gale-force winds swept in during the night, smashing tents and swamping the 15,000 people attending. Thirty people were admitted to hospital suffering from exposure. The two organisers went bankrupt, with a net loss of £31,431.

four

Rishworth

Above: Slitheroe Bridge before it was widened. The house in the centre is the old toll-bar house ideally placed to catch traffic entering the Oldham Turnpike from Bar Lane or Dyson Lane. On the skyline can be seen the chimney of Dyson Mill which was a prominent landmark in the area. Slitheroe Bridge was the boundary between the townships of Rishworth and Soyland.

THE FALLS

THE DERBY

CHURCH OF ST. JOHN THE DIVINE

RISHWORTH

HIGHER BRIDGE, RISHWORTH MOOR

RSH. 14

CUNNING CORNER

Above: Multi-image postcard produced by Lilywhite Ltd, who started out in business in Mill Bank; then, following a disastrous fire at their premises, they moved to Mearclough, Sowerby Bridge. By the time this card was produced they were located in Brighouse.

Right: PC 820 Maloney of the West Riding Constabulary, who was the village bobby for Rishworth for many years. The stripes on his arm were awarded at a rate of one for every five years of service.

Opposite below: Another view of Slitheroe Bridge, taken in the late 1920s or early 1930s. Dyson Lane Mill chimney had been demolished on 8 March 1909. The farm on the right up Dyson Lane is Hoprick Farm, which was operating as a sawmill and timber merchants. The sign on the extreme right, erected by the Lancashire and Yorkshire Railway Co., forbids traction engines and road rollers from using the trestle bridge leading up to Rishworth station.

Above: Goathouse, Rishworth, was built in the seventeenth century and had early connections with the Firth family. It later came into the possession of the Wheelwright family, and it was John Wheelwright who founded Rishworth Grammar School in 1724.

Below: Oldham Road, Rishworth. The man with the dog is identified as Robinson Lumb and the smaller man with the trilby as Sam Darby. Out of sight behind the horse is its owner, Willie Lumb. Further along the road can be seen the Rishworth branch of the Ripponden Co-operative Society.

Right: Beacon (bonfire), on Pike End, Rishworth erected by the Rishworth Urban District Council and set alight on 6 May 1935 to celebrate the Silver Jubilee of the reign of King George and Queen Mary. The bonfire was made from old railway sleepers and was 26ft high. The man in the photograph is William Shepherd, a workman in the employ of the council.

Below: Music festival at Cunning Corner in 1924. The band forming the circle is the Rishworth & Ryburn Valley Brass Band. The white barn next to the Cunning Corner pub was demolished some time ago.

A Lilywhite postcard looking down Oldham Road on Rishworth Moor. On the right is the small Spa Clough Reservoir. On the extreme left can just be seen the roof and chimneys of the Spa Inn, which in 1853 was kept by George Sykes, a gamekeeper. There could well have been a spring of spa water nearby. Today there is no trace of the inn ever having been there.

'The Old Roman Road over Blackstone Edge'. There is little doubt that the route of the old road is Roman, but the jury is still out on whether the surviving stone-set surface is from that period. An earthwork was constructed near here during the English Civil War by the Lancashire Parliamentarians to guard this route over the Pennines from the Royalists.

five

People and Events

This photograph is of Ripponden folk on holiday in the Isle of Man. The peak of the island's tourist industry came in 1899 when there were over 418,000 visitors, many of whom were working-class people from the North of England.

It is 9 August 1902 and the people of Ripponden march along Oldham Road to celebrate the coronation of King Edward VII. The procession is led by the Krumlin Band, followed by the contingent from the Ebenezer Sunday School, Soyland. An old folks' treat was also held at the Royal Hotel, Rishworth.

Above: The delivery wagon from Whiteley's Botanical Brewery of Ripponden, suppliers of soft drinks. One of the family started a similar business in Dundee and may have returned to Ripponden. The Whiteley family kept the Junction Inn until the early 1960s. Drinks such as ginger beer and sparkling hop ale were supplied in stone earthenware bottles.

Right: Mrs Mary Greenwood.

MRS. MARY GREENWOOD.

The above is a picture of Mrs. Mary Greenwood, of 24, Fountain Street, Ripponden, supposed to be 98 years of age, and one of the oldest, if not the oldest, of the residents in the Halifax district. Prior to her marriage to Mr. Abraham Greenwood, of Sowerby, she was engine-tenter and firer-up at Swamp Mill, Sowerby, a handloom weaver, and in domestic service. Afterwards her husband and she kept the Friendly Inn, at Cotton Stones, and, later, two farms in Ripponden and Soyland districts. She has had 15 children. She suffers from a slight deafness, but her activity and mental powers are remarkable.

[By permisson of the *Halifax Courier Ltd.*, Jan. 1907.]

BROADBENT, PRINTER, RIPPONDEN.

The coronation of King George V on 23 June 1911 gave the good people of Ripponden another opportunity to celebrate. The village is festooned with Union Jacks and bunting, and following a service at St Bartholomew's church, a mass singing of hymns was held in the centre of the village.

The procession then led off along Oldham Road, up Dyson Lane and back down Rochdale Road. Each church and chapel provided a contingent such as this one from Stones church. The procession was led by the Heckmondwike English Concertina Band.

Service of Remembrance held at Ripponden war memorial in 1923, no doubt at the eleventh hour of the eleventh day of the eleventh month, which was when the First World War ended (11 November 1918).

Zion church Sunday School Parade with Miss Whiteley in charge. Judging from the style of hats, this is in the 1920s. The enthusiastic waving of the banners by the two boys unfortunately prevents the details being read although the banner towards the rear probably says 'Upward and Onward'.

Above: The first annual sports day held by Ripponden & District School Sports Association, 8 July 1925. The field appears to be Triangle Cricket Club ground. The youngster performing the high jump in the centre of the photograph has unfortunately dislodged the bar.

Left: Charles H. Braund of No. 82 Halifax Road, Ripponden made his living by selling bundles of firewood from his barrow. Firewood was a vital commodity in the days when every house had open coal fires.

Opposite above: Halifax Rugby League Football Club won the Rugby League Challenge Cup at Wembley in 1931 by beating York twenty-two points to eight. This was the first time they had won it since 1904. The cup was paraded around the district and is seen here being led through Ripponden by Rishworth and Ryburn Valley Brass Band on one of their last engagements before being disbanded.

Below: Ripponden Gala, *c.* 1951. This is the Ebenezer Methodist Sunday School (Soyland) float. Some names are known – on the extreme left is Mr Ellis, headmaster of Ripponden School, next are Dorothy Stanley and then Margaret Whitehouse. Kathleen Riley is wearing the sailors cap and to the right of the cowboy is Margaret Whiteley; the girl under the balloon is Joan Morton and the 'King' is Jim Vicars.

The Ripponden Home Guard at their base, Kebroyd Mills, during the Second World War. The Home Guard were originally called the Local Defence Volunteers and were composed of older men, quite often First World War veterans, who were too old to rejoin the regular forces. Their LDV armbands soon attracted derisory interpretations such as 'Long Dentured Veterans', 'Last Desperate Venture' and 'Look Duck and Vanish'. A plan still exists of the positions they would have taken up to defend the centre of Ripponden should the Germans have got this far.

This photograph from around 1956 is said to show the members of Ripponden council in procession to St Bartholomew's church for the annual civic service. In the lead are a police sergeant and special constable.

six

Sport and Leisure

Ripponden Rugby Football Team, 1920/21.

Rishworth Associated Football Team, 1920/21. Taken outside Rishworth National School.

Stones Cricket Team, 1924/25. Taken at Smith Clough House.

Ripponden Pigeon Fanciers' club. Herbert Darby is in the front row, fifth from the left, and Teddy Darby is second from the left on the back row. The Darby family were keepers at Ringstone reservoir for many years.

Rishworth and Ryburn Valley Prize Brass Band, photographed here in 1906 after winning The Daily Graphic Challenge Cup contest held at the Crystal Palace, London:

That Night they wired the village,
Tell, the Ryburn Band has won,
And the lads they all felt bigger,
And the men all said, 'Well done.' (Sam Mellor, local poet)

This fine photograph probably shows the first uniform adopted by the Rishworth and Ryburn Valley band. The band was formed in the 1860s and lasted until the early 1930s, one of the reasons for their demise being the deteriorating condition of their practice room at Slitheroe House. They were known locally as 'The Beer and Baccy Boys' from their favourite Sunday activity of marching from pub to pub, enjoying a smoke and drink at each one. They seem to have had at least three different uniforms during their existence.

The Blackburn Valley Band. The boy at the front is Hubert Wadsworth, who lived at Krumlin.

Ripponden Bowling Club in the early to mid-1950s. Some of the men have been identified – on the back row, from the left: first, Mr Wolstenholme, second, Mr Morton, and third, Arthur Neave. Front row from the left: second, Frank Stanley, third, Mr Morton, and fourth, Tommy Basnet (?).

RIPPONDEN & DISTRICT
BAND OF HOPE UNION.

THE 12th ANNUAL

TEMPERANCE FETE

AND GALA

WILL BE HELD

On the SHOW GROUNDS, LOWER BRIG ROYD,

On Saturday, August 26th, 1893.

SEVEN HOURS' CONTINUOUS PROGRAMME.
OVER EIGHTY PERFORMERS ENGAGED.

INCLUDING THE NOTED

Queen St., Gymnastic Club,

Medallists, from Huddersfield ; Winners of the N.P.R.S. Bronze Challenge
Shield ; Huddersfield and District B.H.U. Silver Challenge Shield, who will
give **ACROBATIC DISPLAYS.**

The RIPPONDEN CORPS of the
St. John Ambulance Brigade

With New Appliances, will give Exhibitions in First Aids : Mimic
Railway Accidents, Drowning, &c.

CONJURING PERFORMANCES BY

PROF. AINSWORTH,

The Renowned Conjuror and Illusionist, in his Classical Entertainment,
WONDERLAND, assisted by **MADAM AINSWORTH.**

Ventriloquism by Prof. GREENWOOD,

With his Comical Dolls, " Dick and Liddy."

PLAITING OF THE MAY POLE,

By 24 beautifully dressed and well-trained Boys and Girls from
St. Peter's B.H., Sowerby.

THE POPULAR HARRISON ROAD
TEMPERANCE ENGLISH CONCERTINA BAND

'Vill Play Selections and Dance Music during the Day.

MONTGOLFIER & GROTESQUE BALLOONS will ascend during the day,

AND AT DUSK, A GRAND

DISPLAY OF FIREWORKS.

GATES OPEN AT 1-30 P.M.
ADMISSION 6d. each; Children Half-price.
GRAND STAND 6d. extra.

Refreshments provided on the Grounds.

CONVENIENT TRAINS & BUSSES RUN EVERY HOUR.

For full particulars see Programmes.   T. RILEY, Secretary.

[SEE OVER.

The Show Grounds
were located where
the car park is now,
opposite the church.

Nowadays, the pupils of Calder Valley High School are the only ones locally who perform the *Peace Egg* play, but at one time it was performed by many other local groups. This photograph shows the troupe of local children who performed the *Peace Egg* play as part of 'Ye Carnival of Merrie England' at the Ripponden Conservative Club in February 1910.

In the days when there was no television or radio, people kept themselves amused by joining groups and societies. Pierrot troupes performing mimes and clown routines were very popular prior to the First World War and here we see the Soyland Pierrot Band.

Concerts and dances were other forms of popular entertainment. This photograph, dated 1901, is of Fred Eastwood's String Band, who were based in Ripponden.

A charabanc waits to take on its load of well-dressed passengers outside the Golden Lion pub at the time when Allan McLean was the licensee. No doubt they are regulars off on a day's excursion. The vehicle bears the name, 'Pioneer – Halifax Motor Carriers'.

seven

Ripponden Co-op

Although the Rochdale Pioneers of 1844 are generally held to be the oldest Co-operative Society, on the 10 November 1832 a meeting was held at the Holroyd Arms (now the Queen Hotel) in Ripponden when it was resolved to form a Co-operative Society. This house in Pleasant Row was rented from Ellis Whiteley and became the first store; 8s 5d were paid for iron bars at the windows. The small room over the passageway was used later as the committee room. The store was soon fitted out and was open from 7 a.m. to 10 p.m. (or 11 p.m. on Saturdays); only members could shop there and membership was limited. Pleasant Row was later acquired by the society and become known locally as 'Co-op Row'.

In 1840 a branch store was opened in Triangle and another was opened at Bolton Brow, Sowerby Bridge in 1847. In 1842, the original store having become too small, the society moved into a larger building next to the Waggon & Horses public house (later renamed the White Swan). By 1860 the society had outgrown this second store and built the Central Stores (shown here) next to it. The previous store then became the Rose & Crown Inn (closed 1911), and then the boot and shoe department of the Co-op, and today it is the Villa Margarita Restaurant. At each end of the new stores was a cottage for each of the storekeepers, but these were incorporated into the store in the 1880s. The shop is now called the 'One Stop Shop'.

The butchery and drapery departments were opened in new premises across the main road from the central stores in 1926. John Crowther, printer, now occupies this building.

This was the Co-op staff when the centenary history of the society was written by J.H. Priestley in 1932. At that time, Whiteley M. Berry was the chairman and Sam Wadsworth was secretary.

Above: Rishworth members had for some time been asking for a branch store in that area and a special meeting was held in May 1892 when it was decided to take over the shop at Lower Godley from Eli Whiteley. Anthony Berry was appointed the manager. The date of this photograph is unknown but the shop staff have been identified as (left to right): Fred Gee, Whiteley Gee and Harold Stansfield. Whiteley Gee subsequently left in 1928 to open his own shop at Kebroyd.

Left: The Dyson Lane branch opened in 1920 in the end house of the row of terraced houses that had been built on the site of the old Dyson Lane Mill. In 1927 a hut was rented at Dyson Lane and the butchery department opened it up every Wednesday for the sale of meat: this may be the same hut which stood in the corner of the field at the bottom of Castle Lane and which later became a fish and chip shop.

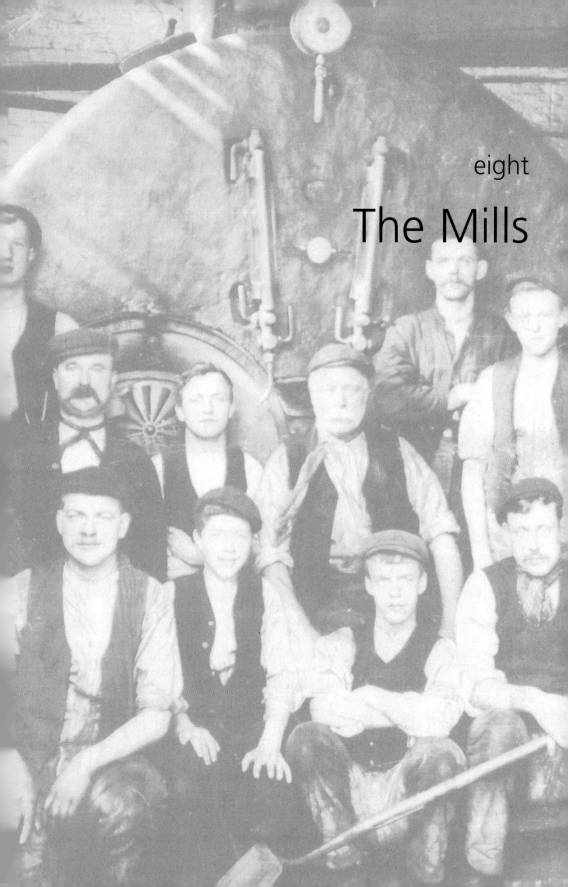

eight

The Mills

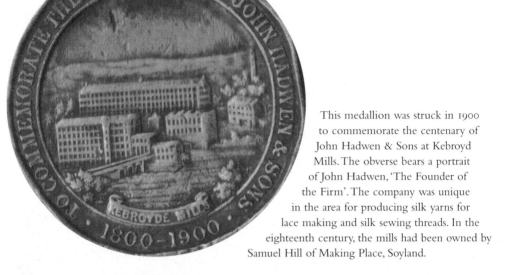

This medallion was struck in 1900 to commemorate the centenary of John Hadwen & Sons at Kebroyd Mills. The obverse bears a portrait of John Hadwen, 'The Founder of the Firm'. The company was unique in the area for producing silk yarns for lace making and silk sewing threads. In the eighteenth century, the mills had been owned by Samuel Hill of Making Place, Soyland.

The winding department at Hadwens. Hadwens went bankrupt in 1901 and 500 workers were thrown out of work; however, a joint stock company took over and continued production, still called 'John Hadwen and Sons'. After the fire of 1904, the mill was rebuilt and silk spinning continued until 1936. This photograph was probably taken in the 1930s. In 1939 the mills were taken over by Blackburn and Sutcliffe as a dye works, but they had to move out when the mills were requisitioned by the Army during the Second World War, and production did not start up again until 1946. The company closed down in 2001.

Hadwens old fire engine at Kebroyd Mills. Fire was an ever-present danger in textile mills, with their oil-soaked floors and flammable raw materials, especially the loose fibre which floated in the air and collected on floors and surfaces. No doubt the old fire engine was pumped with enthusiasm when required and could deal with small fires if the men were on the premises.

This was the scene after the disastrous fire at Kebroyd Mills on Sunday 6 November 1904. A bible was found undamaged in the ruins. There had been previous fires at the mills in 1868 and 1903. Each time the mill was rebuilt, but the end came in May 2006 when the empty mill was completely destroyed by fire while plans were afoot to convert it into flats.

Above: Ripponden Wood Mill (also known as Victoria Mill) was built in 1861 by the Ripponden and District Spinning Company Ltd for the spinning of cotton. Unfortunately, supplies of cotton were limited at the time due to the American Civil War and the company went straight into liquidation; it was purchased by Mr George Whiteley, cotton spinner, of Dyson Lane. The original mill is on the left. The larger one next to it was built in 1916 but demolished in 1988.

Left: Boiler firers at Ripponden Wood Mill: this photograph was taken when the mill was being worked by Meadowcroft and Hampsons, *c.* 1915. After George Whiteley had operated at the mill, it was rented by Lawton Brothers until 1900, and Kaye & Company bought it in 1902.

Opposite above: This rather faded photograph is of a group of textile workers at one of the Ripponden mills, although it has not been possible to identify the premises concerned. The third girl from the left has been identified as Louisa Goulden. Men usually carried out the blending, carding and warehouse jobs as well as being overlookers and mechanics. The majority of mill workers were, however, women; they carried out the spinning, winding and weaving processes.

Below: Ripponden Mill, built in 1876 and known affectionately as 'T' Owd Bass'. It stands on the site of a fourteenth-century fulling mill, which was probably the one leased by the lord of the manor to William Royde or William le Brigg in 1479. Previous mills on the site were destroyed by fire in 1858 and 1876, and on the latter occasion the nearby church belfry was also set on fire by flying sparks. The mill in the photograph is now demolished and the dam drained to form the recreation ground. The Mill Fold development scheme was visited by Prince Charles in June 1991. In the background can be seen Chapel Field Mill.

Above: Aerial view of Commercial Mills, Oldham Road, showing their close proximity to Rishworth railway station on the right; this no doubt influenced the siting of the mills facilitating the shipping in of coal and raw materials, the shipping out of the finished products and the transport of workers from down the valley. At bottom right is the trestle bridge leading up to the station from Slitheroe Bridge, and bottom left is the sawmill which operated at the junction of Dyson Lane and Oldham Road.

Opposite below: There was a fulling mill at Dyson Lane (or Lower Dyson Lane) as early as 1672, and John Hoyle started cotton spinning on the site in 1822. At that time there were two water wheels of 21ft diameter powering the mill. The Ripponden Commercial Co. was started in 1855 as a Co-operative at a time when shareholding was quite an innovation, and it is believed to have been the oldest joint-stock cotton-mill company in Yorkshire. The original six-storey cotton mill was built during the 1860s, but this burnt down in 1880 to be replaced by a new fireproof mill. The adjacent Lower Dyson Lane Mill was purchased in 1927 and incorporated into the mill complex. This photograph was taken from Rishworth station in 1910.

Right: Dyson Lane Mill stood at the top of Dyson Lane, alongside Rochdale Road. It was quite a landmark in the valley being described as 'a city that is set on a hill'. The original mill was built by John Haigh in 1803 and Henry Binns was cotton spinning on the site from the 1820s until 1845 when it was bought by John Whiteley. His son George, who lived at Dyson Field, carried on the business, as did his sons and their Lawton relatives until it closed in 1889.

View from the hillside above Rishworth railway station over Commercial Mills. Dyson Lane Mill can be seen in the top left-hand corner being demolished during 1906-9. The chimney, which had been such a familiar landmark for over sixty years, was felled on 8 March 1909. A row of terraced houses now occupies the site. Note the new houses under construction in Dyson Lane.

Above: Smallees Mill, on the river Ryburn, below Oldham Road, Ripponden, was originally a fulling mill, but was rebuilt as a cotton mill about 1801 by Elkanah Hoyle, a school master, and Joshua Bates, an engineer, with a £1,500 loan from Swaine Brothers' Bank in Halifax. Until 1805 it was rented by Knight and Bamber, cotton spinners from Manchester, and then it was purchased by John Holroyd of Ryburn House, who manufactured fustian cloth there until he died in 1837. It was then taken over by J.W. Wheelwright of Rishworth in 1843. In 1844 the earliest known gas plant in the district was being used to light the mill. It closed down in 1931, and Pancreol Ltd later produced chemicals on the site. It has now been converted into housing.

Left: Another unidentified group of mill girls at one of the local mills. Judging by their dress the photograph was taken in Edwardian times prior to the First World War. Behind them is a creeling frame on which the bobbins of yarn were placed and wound onto a warp beam ready for weaving.

A view looking down Ryburn Dale, *c.* 1925. In the foreground, I believe, is Ryburn Mill, with Stones Mill with its mill dam further along Bar Lane. Beyond Stones Mill can be seen the trestle bridge approach to Rishworth station. Lambert Mill originally stood on the site of Stones Mill and was built around 1800 for cotton spinning by Fenton Lambert & Co. Stones Mill and the original Ryburn Mill were built by John Whiteley in 1855 and 1858 respectively; Stones burnt down in 1882 and was rebuilt the same year. The Whiteley family sold Ryburn Mill to the Ryburn Mill Company Limited in 1894, and Stones Mill closed in 1959.

The abundant water supply in the area made it an ideal location for paper making as well as textiles and there were at least three paper mills in the area over the years. Soyland Paper Mill was established in 1876 by John Leach, a rag merchant, but he went bankrupt after three years. In 1884 Thomas Owen began producing high-class wrapping paper and later newsprint until 1896, when it was taken over by the Ryburndale Paper Mill Co. The mill was completely destroyed by the fire of 25 August 1901 but was rebuilt and back in business by 1903. It finally closed in 1990 and housing has now been built on the site.

Rishworth Mill stands on the site of an old corn mill and malt kiln. The first textile mill was built here in 1836 by Mr Wheelwright. Seen here from Turner Top, the old part of the mill is in the centre of the photograph with Heathfield House, once the home of the Wheelwrights, on the left. At bottom left is Turner Bottom Row which once incorporated the old White Horse Inn. The new mill on the right was built by the Wheelwrights during the 1860s cotton slump, caused by the American Civil War, to keep the unemployed men occupied and to stop them migrating from the area. The new mill originally had a 57.5ft diameter water wheel. The photo dates from 1910.

Left: Young female workers at Spring Mill, Boothwood, taken sometime before 1918, possibly in 1903. Clogs and white pinafores seem to be the order the day. Spring Mill was built at Cunning Corner in around 1800 for the spinning of cotton.

Opposite above: Boothwood Paper Mill at Cunning Corner dates back to 1804 when Scipio Dyson, paper maker of Greetland, was bargaining for water rights with the neighbouring mill owners. The business was taken over in 1808 by William Shepherd and the family business continued producing brown paper until the 1870s; after that, the mill changed hands regularly but continued to make paper. By the 1920s it was being run by a Mr Lockett.

Below: A fire broke out at Boothwood Paper Mill on 6 July 1926 following a smaller one three days before. The mill was completely destroyed, damage being estimated at £10,000. The site was then cleared and was later acquired by the Wakefield Corporation Waterworks, who built Boothwood Reservoir a short distance upstream. Spring Mill can be seen on the right, and above it is the Cunning Corner Inn.

Hanging Lee Mill, or the 'Little Britain' as it was often called, stood just below Rochdale Road and above where Ryburn Reservoir is now. Cotton spinning was taking place on the site as early as 1822, but the mill burnt down in 1865 and was rebuilt by Thomas Wolstenholme & Co. who continued in business until 1897. The premises were then taken over by the Sowerby Bridge & District United Clubs Brewery Co. Ltd from 1908 to 1922. After standing empty for some years after that, the mill was used as a hostel for the workmen building Ryburn reservoir and has since been demolished. The house with the central chimney stack remains.

Bowers Mill in the Blackburn Valley. The Bowers family originated from Bowers Hall on Saddleworth Road; a William Del Bower is known to have witnessed a deed between 1300 and 1330. By 1880 the spinning and doubling mill was being run by B. Taylor & Co., consisting of brothers Ben, Joseph and Sam Taylor. The latter two later took over the mill under the name of J. & S. Taylor, producing woollen cloth.

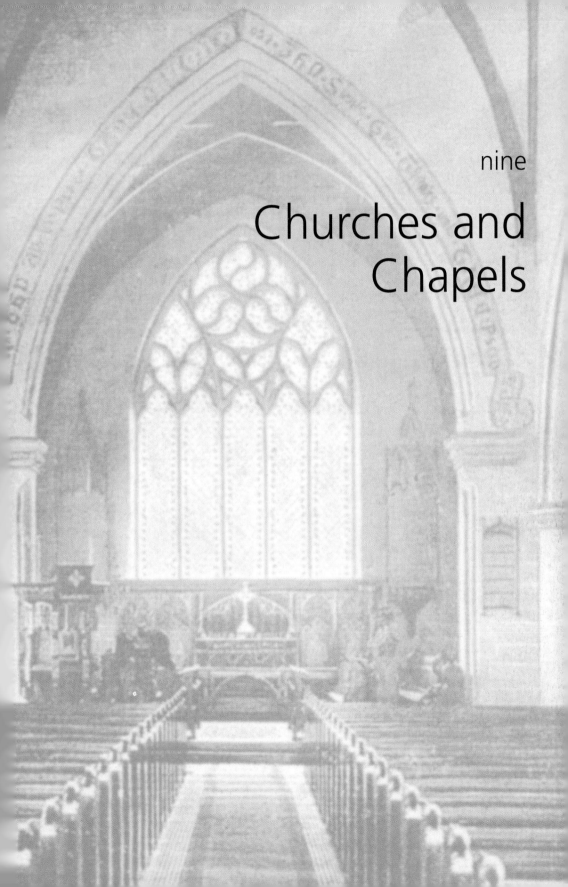

nine

Churches and Chapels

Church and Bridge, Ripponden.

Above: The establishment of the first chapel in
Ripponden was granted by a royal charter signed by
King Edward IV in 1464 and as such is unique in
the Parish of Halifax. It was replaced by the second
chapel in 1610 and by the church in this photograph
in 1729. This third church and its famous yew tree
hedge were demolished in 1867 when the present
St Bartholomew's church was built to replace it. The
pinnacles from the roof of the tower are now in a
garden in the village.

Left: This Lilywhite postcard shows the present church
and its proximity to the old packhorse bridge over
the river Ryburn. The present bridge is thought to
have been rebuilt in the eighteenth century. A great
flood swept down the valley on 18 May 1722, badly
damaging the 1610 church and washing bodies out of
the graveyard. After the flood had subsided, one coffin
was found jammed in a tree; several mills, cottages
and bridges were swept away and many people were
drowned.

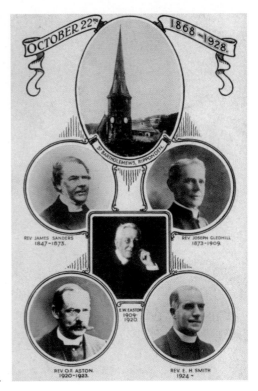

Right: This postcard was produced in 1928 to celebrate the diamond jubilee (sixty years) of the building of the present church. It depicts the five vicars appointed to the church during that period.

Below: Interior view of St Bartholomew's church. The stained-glass windows still incorporate small sections of glass from the original medieval church. Some of the pillars from the third church, demolished in 1867, were reused in the present one.

This photograph, taken in around 1920, shows the Revd O.F. Astin (seated middle of second row) and the choir of St Bartholomew's church. The boy, front row fourth from right, is Luther Neave (known as Dick), whose father, George William Neave, was the stationmaster at Ripponden railway station. They lived at Rockery Cottage.

Christ Church, Barkisland, was built in 1854 to supply the needs of the growing population. It was consecrated by the Bishop of Ripon at its opening. The Barkisland war memorial stands nearby.

Lighthazles (Methodist New Connection) Chapel in Soyland was established by a break-away group from Stones Wesleyan church in 1816. A vestry was added in 1862 over the door of which the words 'Union is Strength – and Friendship is Sweet' were inscribed. Prior to 1868 it was the custom for men to sit on the left of the chapel and women on the right. The chapel was demolished some time ago but the 1862 vestry section with the above inscription over the door still stands.

Ebenezer (Methodist New Connection) Chapel at Soyland Town was also formed as the result of the 1816 split from Stones Wesleyan church. The first chapel was built in 1818, and Mr Dove, from Making Place College just round the corner, attended the chapel on Sunday mornings to teach reading and writing. The chapel in the photograph was built in 1880 at a cost of £16,000, but today only the railings and gates survive.

Above: Zion Congregational Chapel in Oldham Road, Ripponden was formed in 1868 by a group who left Rishworth Baptist church after some dissention there. The new chapel was opened in 1870 and the fairytale design has been credited to Mr R.K. Lee of Kebroyd House. Ripponden Technical Institute started in a classroom here in 1891.

Below: The interior of Zion Chapel, which had a seating capacity of 450, was badly damaged by a fire on 29 April 1902 and repairs took a year to complete at a cost of £564. The new organ, installed by W. Andrews of Bradford, cost £350.

Zion Congregational Church,

RIPPONDEN.

MEN'S SERVICE

ON SUNDAY AFTERNOON,

February 9th, 1908, at 3-15 prompt.

SPEAKER:

REV. ALBERT WOOD,

OF TRIANGLE.

SUBJECT:

"The Man who was too busy to do his work."

Chairman := MR. W. WHITELEY, RIPPONDEN.

Elocutionist :- MISS M. L. NICHOL, Ripponden.

COLLECTION TO DEFRAY EXPENSES.

ALL MEN ARE WELCOME.

[See over—Hymns for Service.

W. H. Broadbent, Printer, Ripponden

Male members of Zion Chapel: no doubt some of them attended the Men's Service on the previous page, and listened to the Revd Wood's talk on 'The man who was too busy to do his work'. A Young Men's Mutual Improvement Society had been established at the chapel in 1870.

The Non-Conformist movement began to take root towards the end of the eighteenth century, and by 1800 Ripponden Baptists had to walk the five or six miles to Steep Lane Baptist church, above Sowerby, to attend the Sunday service. A new congregation was formed in Rishworth, and the Baptist Chapel was built in 1803. Two nearby cottages were purchased in 1812 and converted into a Sunday School, which expanded with a new three-storey building being built in the gap between the chapel and the cottages joining them all together. The three-storey building has since been demolished and the chapel itself has now been converted into a private dwelling.

This new purpose-built Sunday School was erected in 1897 to the rear of Rishworth Baptist Chapel. Movable partitions divided the interior up into classrooms, but once removed an assembly hall for 350 persons was created.

Male members of the Rishworth Baptist's congregation photographed outside the Manse (Ministers House) in Rishworth New Road. The Manse was built in 1887 at a cost of £550. A Mutual Improvement Society had been established in 1853.

Above: Krumlin Methodist Chapel was built in 1868 on land at 'Calf Garth' largely from the support of Mr John Hoyle, the owner of Krumlin Mill, who lived at Krumlin Hall. Prior to the chapel being built, meetings were held in a storeroom at the mill. Krumlin had a much larger population in those days, and 123 children attending the Sunday school were being taught by twenty-five teachers. By 1968 there were only four children attending and the whole congregation only numbered twenty-two adults.

Above: Laying the foundation stone at St John's church, Rishworth; the stone reads, 'In the Faith of Jesus Christ – This Stone was set by J.R.H. Wheelwright Esq on the 28th day of May 1927'.

Below: Church of St John the Divine, Godley Lane(!), Rishworth. The sod-cutting ceremony to commence building took place on 2 April 1927. The lych gate, added in 1938, is an unusual feature of churches in the area.

Opposite below: St Matthew's church, Oldham Road, Cunning Corner, was erected in 1890 to ease the pressure on the small chapel at Goathouse (now the chapel for Rishworth School). Built of galvanised sheet iron over a wooden frame, the church was known locally as the 'Iron Church' or the 'Tin Tabernacle' (or the 'Tin Tab'). St Matthew's was closed in 1927 and dismantled by a Mr Taylor of Fox Stones, who paid £25 for it in 1928.

This is the original Stones Wesleyan Chapel, which opened in 1804. 'At the prayer meetings, two or three of the brethren would be moved to pray all at once, and the shouting of praise would become louder and louder, until it was impossible to hear the words of any one of them. The emotion was great and the hour thus spent seemed as a few minutes'. Peter Gledhill was the caretaker and schoolmaster for over thirty-five years. He lived in the two-roomed chapel house at the rear and constructed the sundial above the door.

By the end of the nineteenth century the old Stones Chapel was showing signs of decay and the decision was taken to replace it. The new chapel, pictured here, was built alongside the old one and opened for worship in 1902, following which the old chapel was demolished and the ground incorporated into the graveyard. One remarkable gravestone records the death of Sarah, wife of Joseph Crawshaw. She died in 1844, aged eighty-nine years, and 'was mother, grandmother, great grandmother and gt. great grandmother to 397 children'.

ten

Schools

BARKISLAND GRAMMAR SCHOOL,

NEAR RIPPONDEN.

MR. ROUSE receives Pupils to be Instructed in the usual Branches of a Liberal Education.

TERMS.

	£.	s.	d.	
Board for Pupils under 12 years of Age	18	0	0	℈ Annum.
„ „ above 12	22	0	0	ditto
Weekly Board for Pupils under 12	15	0	0	ditto
„ „ above 12	19	0	0	ditto
Instruction, including the Classics, the English Language, Writing, Arithmetic, Elements of the Mathematics, Geography, &c.	4	4	0	ditto
Washing	2	0	0	ditto

FRENCH, &c. ON THE USUAL TERMS.

BEFORE THE REMOVAL OF A PUPIL, A QUARTER'S NOTICE IS EXPECTED.

This School has been Fourteen Years successfully conducted by the present Master, who, if applied to, can give numerous and satisfactory References to Gentlemen whose sons have been educated by him both for Professional and Commercial Pursuits. The Pupils receive every care and domestic comfort which a Parent can require. The salubrity of this neighbourhood, the purity of its atmosphere and water, render the situation of the School well adapted to promote a healthy and robust constitution.

Advertisement from *Walkers Directory* of the Parish of Halifax, 1845. There were several private boarding schools in the area, including Parkfield in Blue Ball Lane, off Rochdale Road, which took in boarders from 1847 until the 1890s.

A class at Barkisland School, 1919. The teacher is Miss Whitworth and the headmaster is Mr Moores.

Ripponden National School, *c.* 1900. The headmaster is Mr Clements. The first part of the school, in Elland Road, was built in 1843 and was gradually extended over the years, the playground not being added until 1910. When the new school was built at Brig Royd in 1980, this old school became a keep-fit gymnasium, and in 1996 it was converted into housing.

Rishworth National School in the 1930s. The girl third from the left on the back row is Ivy Taylor, sister of Donald Taylor who has provided many of the photographs in this book. The school opened in 1874.

The Wesleyan Day School at Stones, Rochdale Road. The school was built in 1886 on land purchased from Joseph Whiteley of Stones House. The photograph is from a postcard and was taken prior to 1918. Note the girl with the hoop and stick – a popular game at the time.

Stones School, 1921. A photograph of the handful of school children who had not missed a day at school that year. The school closed in 1980.

Commercial College, Making Place Hall, Soyland, 1838. Previously the home and business premises of Samuel Hill, one of Yorkshire's wealthiest clothiers, Making Place was opened as a private boarding college by William Dove in 1832 with twelve pupils. By the 1860s it had 200 scholars and a staff of twenty masters. It declined after the death of Mr Dove in 1865 and closed in 1880. One boy by the name of Asquith later became Prime Minister.

A game of cricket in progress in the field opposite the college, and a cow seems to have stopped play! Subjects taught at the college included arithmetic, history, geography, surveying, German, engineering, French, classics, perspective drawing and shorthand. The school even produced its own gas supply and had its own hospital. On Sundays the staff and boys would march down to St Bartholomew's church for the service, and a stained-glass window there, in memory of Mr Dove, was donated by the students.

This is the original Rishworth Grammar School, founded and endowed in 1724 by John Wheelwright for the education of his tenant's children. The building served as the school for over 100 years with the pupils boarding at nearby Goathouse. When the new school was built this old building was used as a joiner's shop until 1839 and then as a chapel for the people of Rishworth until the 1920s, when it became the chapel for Rishworth School.

Staff and pupils at Rishworth School, taken in 1909. The headmaster at this time was R.H. Elliot, who was appointed in 1878 and continued in the post until his retirement, aged eighty-seven, in 1919. The school was boys only from 1921 until 1968, when girls were re-admitted.

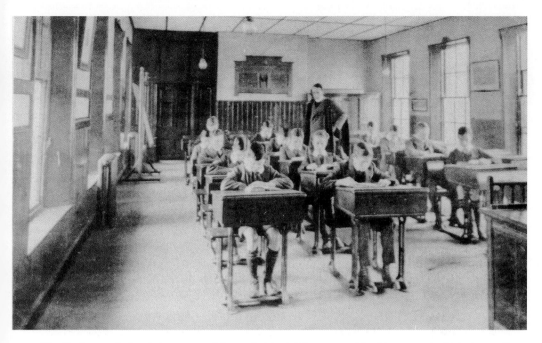

The bleakness of school classrooms of the period is vividly portrayed in this postcard which the pupils at Rishworth School could purchase at the school shop to send home to their families. The teacher is believed to be C.E.B. Kingsford.

View of the 'new' Rishworth School built in the Georgian style in 1828 (and later added to in the neo-Georgian style in 1930). By 1843 there were seventy pupils and by the middle of the nineteenth century it was described as the richest educational foundation in Yorkshire with excellent premises. Heathfield House was bought in 1950 as a preparatory school. Today Rishworth is a thriving independent school.

Rishworth School formed a Combined Cadet Force in 1923. They were equipped with seventy old Lee Enfield carbines of Boer War vintage, on loan from the War Office. They did arms drill, square bashing, and route marches, trained on the rifle range and went to camps abroad as well as in the UK such as this one at Redcar in 1935. The CCF was disbanded in 1963.

Rishworth Grammar School Scouts, 47th Halifax Brigade, photographed at Rishworth station.

eleven

Pubs

Above: The Old Bridge Inn, probably the most photographed pub in the Ryburn Valley. It was renamed The Waterloo (or Old Waterloo Inn) shortly after that famous battle in 1815, but later reverted to its original name. One of Yorkshire's oldest inns, it is mentioned in records as far back as 1307. The Ripponden stocks were re-erected here at the end of the packhorse bridge after being moved from their original position opposite the Golden Lion pub. This photograph was taken in around 1865. The stocks were dismantled and taken away in 1887 and no one thought to preserve them.

Left: It was customary to whitewash the internal walls of the pub each year and a piece of whitewash examined in 1882 revealed over 250 layers. One of the most famous landladies was 'Ruth o' t' Waterloo', who left in the 1870s to marry Robert Holt, a partner in Chapel Field Mill. She might well be the lady in the photograph believed to have been taken in the 1860s. The pub figures in several incidents in Phyllis Bentley's novel *Manhold* and must be unique today in having no pub sign outside.

The Golden Lion Inn from an advertising card dating to the end of the nineteenth century when R. Waring was the proprietor. The pub is described as 'a family and commercial hotel with billiard and concert rooms, good stabling and carriages kept for hire'. 'Omnibuses arrive and depart at short intervals'. The telephone number was '040 Rishworth'.

The Golden Lion, 1918, the Union Jack no doubt flying to celebrate victory in the First World War. The pub was once known as 'The Spout' after the adjacent old Spout Farm, the first mention of which is in 1673. First reference to a pub here is in 1754. The extension on the right, now demolished, was once a dining room and also a reading room where newspapers could be read. The post office was located here until the 1840s. The sign over the door shows George W. Kershaw as the landlord and the two people have been identified as Mrs Stansfield and her son.

The Queen Hotel was built in around 1800 on the new turnpike road. Originally called The Stansfield Arms, in 1819 it was 'The Prince of Orange'; by 1825 it was known as 'The Prince William Inn'. New owners, soon afterwards, renamed it 'The Holroyd Arms', but in 1856 it again changed to 'The Queens Arms'. By the time of the photograph (around 1905), it had reverted to 'The Queen Hotel' again, James Booth being the landlord. The Queen was for many years the meeting place of the Ripponden Female Society. The Golden Lion is in the background.

The Commercial Inn, Oldham Road: a party of regulars is about to set off on a pub trip in the 1950s. The coach driver stands second from the left, and no doubt the coach was on hire from Ripponden and District Motors which was next to the pub. As can be seen, the pub sold Ramsdens' Stone Trough Ales, which were brewed in Halifax from 1735 until bought out by Joshua Tetley's in 1964. The pub is now called 'The Besom'. The pub was originally built as 'Glenhaven Cottage' in 1860.

The Royal Hotel, Rishworth, from a postcard dated 1908. This is another pub built in 1799 to service traffic on the new turnpike road. It was originally called 'The Kings Arms' and the first landlord was Thomas Leach of Halifax. Rishworth councillors held their meetings here for a time, as did the Manchester Unity of Oddfellows. The pub is now called 'The Old Malthouse'.

The Spread Eagle Inn in Heys Lane, behind Rishworth Mill. In 1800 it was known as the Butts Green, an alehouse kept by James Rainforth deriving its name from the nearby archery butts where local archers were compelled to practice during medieval and Tudor times. At the time the photograph was taken, Sarah Schofield was the licensee, until she left in the 1930s. The well-dressed group of men may be local councillors. The sign in the window shows it to be another Ramsdens' pub; it closed in 1948 and is now a private house.

The Cunning Corner Inn, Rishworth, from an old postcard, another inn built on the roadside of the new turnpike road where previously no road had existed. In the 1840s it was named the Coach and Horses, and in 1857 the Oddfellows Arms (being the local HQ of that order). By 1874, John Holroyd was running his horse-drawn haulage business from here. The pub has recently been renamed 'The Old Bore'.

The Derby Inn, Oldham Road, Rishworth, when Alexander George Henley was the licensee. This old coaching inn was once the property of Lord Savile, who also owned Rishworth Lodge on the hillside above. A favourite stopping place for wagonettes and week-end trippers, it was renowned for its ham-and-egg teas and was a Temperance hotel (no alcohol) for a time in the late 1800s. Lord Savile closed it down as a patriotic gesture during the First World War and had difficulty obtaining a licence afterwards. It has recently been called 'the Exit 22' due to its proximity to that junction on the M62, but is now called The Turnpike.

The White Hart, Rochdale Road, was here long before the road was constructed past it. It bears the date 1630 and was partly built by the Whiteley family. A 'hart' was a type of deer. On the extreme left is the boundary wall of Dyson Mill, with the Butchers Arms pub beyond. The row of terraced houses adjoining the White Hart has now been demolished and the pub itself closed in the 1990s and is now divided into dwellings. Peter Rigby Wood was the landlord when this photograph was taken in around 1900.

The Butchers Arms, Rochdale Road, originally occupied only this end of the row of cottages but has gradually expanded to take in the whole block. It was named after the abattoir that formally stood to the right of the pub. The man in the doorway is probably the landlord, John Atkinson.

The New Inn, Rochdale Road, Baitings, was built in around 1750 to replace the Blue Ball Inn, which was now bypassed on the old road above. Both pubs continued to trade until recently, but now both are closed and converted to houses. This photo is from a postcard sent from Barkisland in 1931. The sundial over the right-hand door still survives.

Although just 'over the border' in Lancashire, the White House pub is well known to residents of the Ryburn Valley. This view is from a postcard sent to Bethel Terrace, Norland, in 1906. Built in 1671, this old coaching house, originally called the Coach and Horses, was where 'the young bloods of Littleborough having guarded the mail coach from highwaymen would seek recompense for their labours with vigorous application to strong liquors'.

twelve

Transport

A team of horses rest and enjoy a feed from their nose bags outside the Golden Lion Inn, *c.* 1900. No doubt the driver was enjoying liquid refreshment inside.

Taken next to a weighbridge at either Ripponden or Rishworth railway stations, this photograph shows the horse and cart belonging to Levi Lumb, coal merchant of Ripponden. His load, however, appears to be logs.

The Derby Delph Disaster, Saturday 7 April 1906. Whilst travelling along Oldham Road, the young horse pulling this trap suddenly shied away from a sheep, crashed through the boundary wall and plunged into the quarry (delph) below. Three men from Oldham, all called William (William Shaw, William Smithies and William Kenworthy), were killed instantly, whilst a fourth was badly injured.

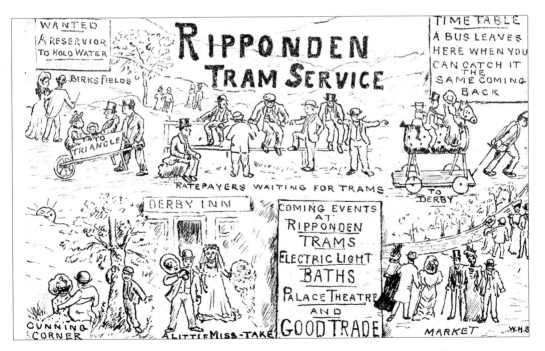

A humorous postcard dated 1905 listing facilities yet to be enjoyed by Ripponden ratepayers, with a special moan about the lack of a tram service which got no closer than Triangle. The message on the card reads – 'how do you like busy Ripponden?'

Leyland ex-Army wagon owned by Arthur Holmes, 1920. Mr Holmes is said to be the driver at the wheel and his wife is standing at the corner of the building. He used the vehicle as a haulage wagon during the week and then bolted on the seating section to take out charabanc parties at the weekend.

Above: Beaumont Brothers were specialists in heavy haulage. They were based at Ripponden Garage and Manchester House, Ripponden, telephone number 28! They also had premises in Bradford. The photograph is taken outside the Derby Bar, Rishworth.

Opposite: The table of toll charges from the toll gate located at Slitheroe Bridge. This is a piece of slate measuring 5ft by 3ft, which has recently been found, being used as a table in the cellar of a house in Ripponden. Oldham Road was made at the beginning of the nineteenth century by the Oldham and Ripponden Trust and the toll bars were removed on 1 November 1883. One toll that can still be read states that 'for every horse or other beast drawing any cart or other such carriage with two wheels of the breadth of 6in or upward at the bottom of the sole thereof – 4d'.

Ripponden railway station. The Rishworth Branch Railway was opened from Sowerby Bridge to Ripponden on 5 August 1878 by the Lancashire and Yorkshire Railway. Ripponden people were 'delirious with joy at having at last the trains on their doorstep'. When the first train arrived at the gaily decorated station, a cannon was fired, the church bells were rung, and the locals, given the day off work from the local mills, enjoyed open house at the local inns. Over 2,000 people travelled on the line that day.

Motor trains consisting of a small engine and carriage combined in one unit were brought into use on the line in 1907. Rail motor No. 11, with the 'Sowerby Bridge & Rishworth' nameplate on the roof, is pictured here while being used on the Stainland branch line. They were affectionately known in the Ryburn Valley as the 'Rishworth Pigs'.

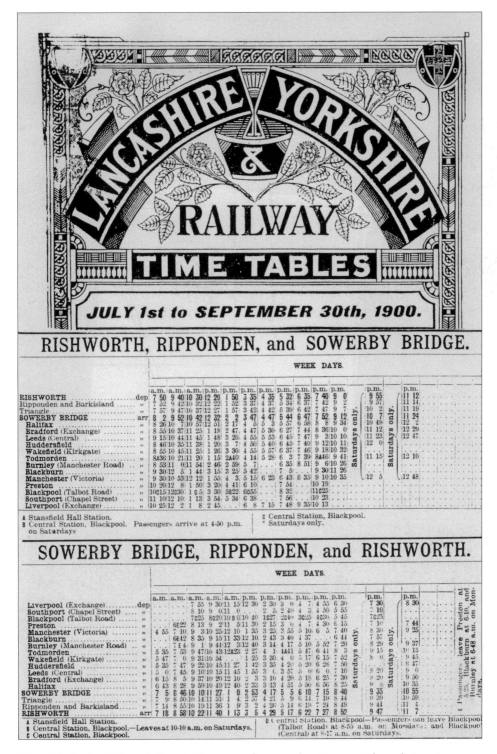

Timetable for the Rishworth Branch Line, 1900. If you caught a train in Rishworth at 7.50 a.m. you could be in Blackpool by 10.15 a.m. – not bad for 1900!

Rishworth railway station. The line was opened as far as Rishworth (Slitheroe Bridge) on 1 March 1881. There were plans to continue the line to Littleborough by tunnelling under Blackstone Edge, but these were abandoned and Rishworth became the end of the line. There was a busy goods yard here with coal and cotton being brought in and yarn, cloth and paper being shipped out.

Rail motor No. 5, and railway staff at Rishworth station, photographed in 1909. The journey back to Sowerby Bridge would take twelve minutes, the train being reversed with the driver using a set of controls at the rear of the coach. The coach could seat fifty-six passengers and 'the smoker has to forego his weed… but the journey is not a lengthy one.'

The trestle bridge, built in 1880 to connect Rishworth Station with Oldham Road at Slitheroe Bridge. It was 20ft wide and paved with stone setts. The nearest chimney belongs to Slitheroe Paper Mill, with those of Stones Mill and Lower Swift Place Mill in the distance. In the trees on the right is Stones House and Stones church is on the skyline. The trestle bridge was demolished in 1953.

A saddle-tank locomotive, which seems to be pulling a combined passenger and goods train, near the Watson Mill Lane crossing in 1911.

The last train to use the Rishworth Branch Line leaving Watson Mill Lane crossing on its way to Ripponden on 1 September 1958: the line had closed to passenger traffic in September 1929 and goods trains went no further than Ripponden after 1952.

One of the main causes of the demise of the Rishworth Branch Railway was the increasing popularity and convenience of road transport. John Hirst Sr founded Ripponden & District Motors in 1921, running single-decker buses between Rishworth, Halifax and Elland. This photograph shows the Elland bus at the top of Elland Road with the Golden Lion in the background. The crew are wearing their summer uniforms.

This 'mini-bus' of its day was rescued from a farmyard and renovated by staff at Ripponden and District Motors. It was painted royal blue, and took part in many vintage rallies, hence the number '44' in the windscreen. The engine is being tuned outside the company garage in Oldham Road.

Three busloads of Ripponden folk about to set off on a day's excursion in 1931. By this time Ripponden and District Motors had extended their routes to Manchester, Oldham and Denshaw. Mr John Hirst, the founder of the company, stands near the front of the first coach wearing a bowler hat; his son, John Hirst Jr, later to become managing director, is on the left of Mr Hirst's group. The coaches are Leyland Tigers and the driver at far left has been identified as Priestley Barrett.

Above: Buses No. 11 and No. 12, probably brand new, stand on Slitheroe Bridge for a photo shoot. If you wanted to book an excursion the number to ring was Ripponden 97!

Left: A crew of one of the R&D buses in 1931, wearing the winter uniform. Seated is the driver, Percy Shepherd, and standing is the conductor, Richard Whitehouse.

A 1952 AEC Mark IV with rare half-deck body, photographed on delivery to the company outside Ripponden and District Motors, Oldham Road, Ripponden. The coach was painted metallic blue and grey.

This Leyland Titan was one of at least two double-deckers operated by R&D. It was purchased by the company in 1930 and was one of the five vehicles transferred to the Halifax Joint Omnibus Committee when R&D's bus services were bought out by them for £12,000 in 1934. Two years later this bus was sold to Western SMT in Kilmarnock, Scotland.

A Leyland Bison wagon from 1932, shortly after R&D moved into the parcel delivery business. The blue and cream wagons became a familiar sight in the local area. The coaching side of the company's activities finally ended in the late 1950s.

Ripponden & District operated their own recovery vehicle, seen here on the moors above Rishworth. A snow plough could be attached. The company later changed its name to Ripponden Carriers and in 1999 it was taken over by a management buyout and subsequently moved out of the area.

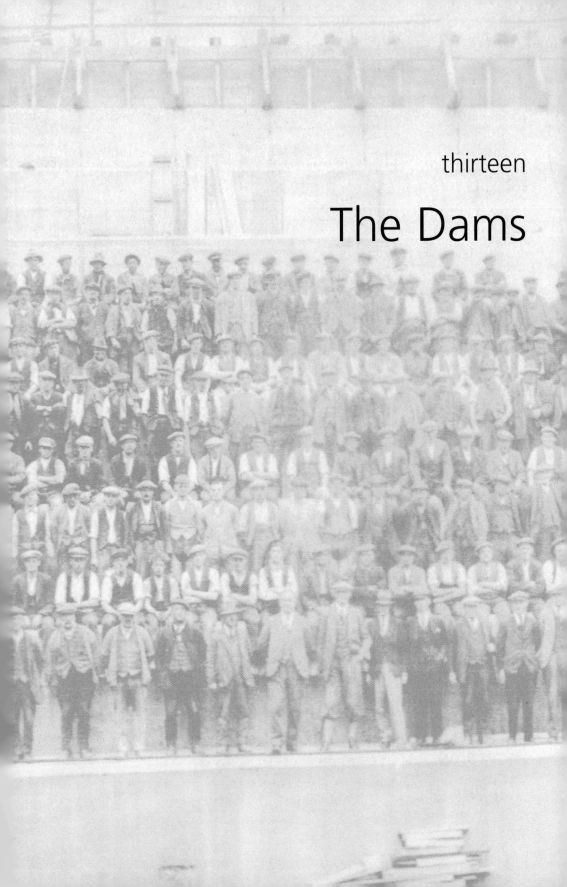

thirteen

The Dams

"Farewell to Bogden".

RPN. 37.   COPYRIGHT VIEWS BY   LILYWHITE LD., COTTONSTONES.

THE ABOVE VIEWS CONSTITUTE BOGDEN VALLEY IN 1924.
THE WHOLE OF THIS SCENERY WILL BE OBLITERATED DURING 1925 AND FOR EVER AFTERWARDS ON
ACCOUNT OF THE CONVERSION OF THE WHOLE DISTRICT INTO A RESERVOIR FOR THE WAKEFIELD CORPORATION.

Above: These views were taken of Ryburn Valley in 1924, prior to the building of Ryburn Reservoir which was going to flood that part of the valley, known locally as Bogden. The area had long been a favourite beauty spot for walks and picnics and the sentiment 'Farewell to Bogden' was shared by all local people. The postcard was produced by Lilywhites of Cottonstones, Mill Bank.

Left: A party poses on one of the soon-to-be submerged bridges, *c.* 1900. Local poet Whiteley Lumb was moved to write the following words in 1925:

Sweet Bogden, thou art dear to me,
I write thy name with grateful tears,
And bid a sad farewell to thee,
Thou bonny gem of former years.

Right: The building of Ryburn Dam was authorised by an Act of Parliament of 1924 to provide water for the City of Wakefield. Here we see Alderman John Tennant JP wheeling away the first sod cut to start work on Ryburn Reservoir, 15 July 1925, applauded by councillors and officials from Wakefield Corporation.

Below: Ryburn Dam wall under construction in September 1928, looking north towards Rochdale Road: the light-coloured Stansfield Hey farmhouse was converted into a boardroom, office and home for the resident engineer and First World War huts were erected on site to house some of the workforce. The 2ft gauge railway line from Hanging Lee quarry runs on to the gantry feeding the concrete mixer. The building of the dam attracted busloads of local people to picnic and watch the work in progress.

Above: The workforce at Ryburn reservoir line up for a photograph on the steps of the nearly finished dam wall on 12 June 1930: I make it 215 men, and nearly every one wearing a flat cap! The dam was opened on 7 September 1933 by Councillor A. Hopkinson, chairman of the Wakefield Waterworks Committee.

Left: A rather poor-quality photograph of 'Civil Bill', a ganger (sub foreman) who worked on the Boothwood dams amongst others. Giving nicknames to fellow workers was a practice that went back to the canal and railway-building days of the nineteenth century. Others that worked on the Booth Dean schemes are recorded as: 'Bible Punching Joey', 'Cambridge Lion', 'Mad Cumberland', Nottingham Tom', 'Stocking-knitting Bob' and 'Sumphole Lank'.

Baitings Dam under construction. Work started in 1948 by the Wakefield City Waterworks Dept, and it took six years to complete. 375,000 tons of concrete were used and the dam wall is 200ft high. It covers 64 acres and can hold 775 million gallons of water to a maximum depth of 155ft. It was officially opened on 14 November 1956 by the Mayor of Wakefield, Councillor A.G. Webster JP.

Postcard of the completed dam taken from behind the New Inn. The new viaduct, which cost £50,000, at the far end of the reservoir carries the 'Back o' th' Height' road to Parrock Nook and Rishworth; it replaced the old bridge which can still be seen when the water level is low. Since this photograph was taken the Water Board has planted thousands of trees around the reservoir.

Other local titles published by Tempus

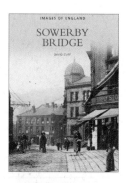

Sowerby Bridge
DAVID CLIFF

This excellent selection of old photographs shows the famous Yorkshire textile town of Sowerby Bridge, from its heyday of industrial importance through to post-industrial, late twentieth-century times. Fascinating scenes of everyday life are pictured; from children at school to the many activities that took place in and around the churches and from workers in factories to domestic views of home. The book will appeal to all who know and love this area.

978 0 7524 3772 9

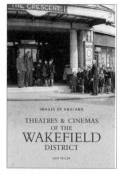

Theatres and Cinemas of the Wakefield District
KATE TAYLOR

Through the medium of old photographs, programmes and advertisements, this splendid collection provides a fascinating look at the history of theatre- and cinema-going in Wakefield and its adjacent towns over the last century. Including insights into the technology behind the silver screen, the entrepreneurs and the cinema chains who operated in the area, *Theatres and Cinemas of the Wakefield District* reveals how the experience of cinema-going has changed over the decades.

978 0 7524 4281 5

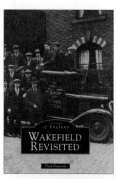

Wakefield Revisited
PAUL DAWSON

The city of Wakefield rose to national prominence in 1889 when it became the county town of the West Riding of Yorkshire. The photographs in this diverse and fascinating selection reflect the physical fabric of the town, and offer a unique insight into the people's social, political, economic and diverse cultural heritage. Older residents will enjoy this trip down memory lane and those who have not known Wakefield for long will find an insight into Wakefield never seen before.

978 0 7524 2491 0

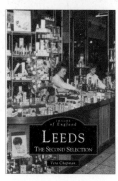

Leeds: The Second Selection
VERA CHAPMAN

In this superb collection of images, historic Leeds is revealed to the reader through a remarkable selection of postcards and archive photographs. Vera Chapman has collated pictures that defy the traditional image of industrial cities, and instead shows Leeds with a profusion of parks, statuary and grand buildings. *Leeds: The Second Selection* will delight those who know the area, evoking memories of former times.

978 0 7524 2650 1

If you are interested in purchasing other books published by Tempus, or in case you have difficulty finding any Tempus books in your local bookshop, you can also place orders directly through our website

www.tempus-publishing.com